CIMA

Risk Management

Strategic level | Subject P3

CIMA's official revision cards

AF875254

KAPLAN PUBLISHING

Published by: Kaplan Publishing UK

Unit 2 The Business Centre, Molly Millars Lane,
Wokingham, Berkshire RG41 2QZ

Acknowledgements
The AICPA & CIMA Publishing trademark is reproduced with kind permission of CIMA.

British Library Cataloguing in Publication Data

A catalogue record for this book is available from the British Library

ISBN 978-1-83735-117-6

Printed and bound in Great Britain

RISK MANAGEMENT

Kaplan Publishing's learning materials are designed to help students succeed in their examinations.
In certain circumstances, CIMA can make post-exam adjustment to a student's mark or grade to reflect adverse circumstances which may have disadvantaged a student's ability to take an exam or demonstrate their normal level of attainment (see CIMA's Special Consideration policy). However, it should be noted that students will not be eligible for special consideration by CIMA if preparation for or performance in CIMA's CGMA exams are affected by any failure by their tuition provider to prepare them properly for the exam for any reason including, but not limited to, staff shortages, building work or a lack of facilities etc.

Similarly, CIMA will not accept applications for special consideration on any of the following grounds:

- failure by a tuition provider to cover the whole syllabus
- failure by the student to cover the whole syllabus, for instance as a result of joining a course part way through
- failure by the student to prepare adequately for the exam, or to use the correct pre-seen material
- errors in the Kaplan Official Study Text, including sample (practice) questions or any other Kaplan content or
- errors in any other study materials (from any other tuition provider or publisher).

How to use Revision Cards

The concept

- Revision Cards are a new and different way of learning, based upon research into learning styles and effective recall.
- The cards are in full colour and have text supported by a range of images, making them far more effective for visual learners and easier to remember.
- Unlike a bound text, Revision Cards can be rearranged and reorganised to appeal to kinaesthetic learners who prefer to learn by doing.
- Being small enough to carry around means that you can take them anywhere. This gives the opportunity to keep going over what you need to learn and so helps with recall.
- The content has been reduced down to the most important areas, making it far easier to digest and identify the relationships between key topics.
- Revision Cards, however you learn, whoever you are, wherever you are.........

How to use them

Revision Cards are a pack of approximately 52 cards, slightly bigger than traditional playing cards but still very easy to carry and so convenient to use when travelling or moving around. They can be used during the tuition period or at revision.

They are broken up into 3 sections.

- An overview of the entire subject in a mind map form (orange).
- A mind map of each specific topic (blue).
- Content for each topic presented so that it is memorable (green).

Each one is a different colour, allowing you to sort them in many ways.

- Perhaps you want to get a more detailed feel for each topic, why not take all the green cards out of the pack and use those.
- You could create your own mind maps using the blue cards to explore how different topics fit together.
- And if there are some topics that you understand, take those out of the pack, leaving yourself only the ones you need to concentrate on.

There are just so many ways you can use them.

Contents

Exam guidance

Your exam will be made up of 60 questions, covering every area of the syllabus.

A range of question types will be used. The main types will be: multiple choice, multiple response, number entry, drag and drop, drop down and select all that apply.

All questions are equally weighted and independent of each other.

All elements of a question must be answered correctly for the question to be marked correct.

The pass mark is a scaled score of 100.

Time allowed: 90 minutes. No extra time is given for reviewing your answers.

Core areas of the syllabus

A	Enterprise risk	25%
B	Strategic risk	25%
C	Internal controls	25%
D	Cyber risks	25%

Quality and accuracy are of the utmost importance to us so if you spot an error in any of our products, please send an email to mykaplanreporting@kaplan.com with full details, or follow the link to the feedback form in MyKaplan.

Our Quality Co-ordinator will work with our technical team to verify the error and take action to ensure it is corrected in future editions.

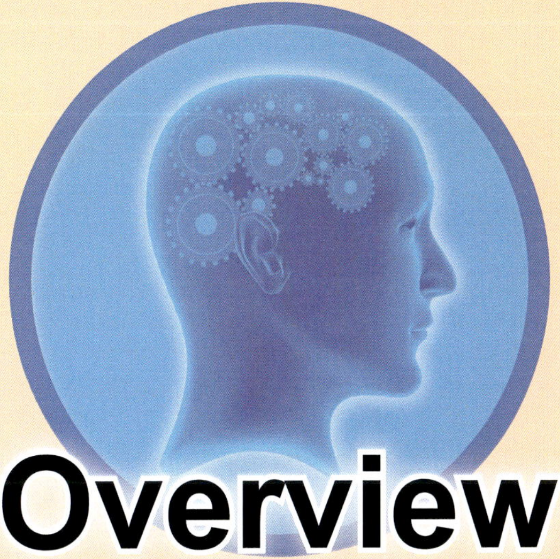

Overview

risk management

RevisionCards

Types
and sources
Risk
management
Enterprise risk
Strategy risk
Ethics
Governance
Strategic risk
Risk
Management
Reputational risk
Cyber security
processes
Cyber threats
Control systems
Cyber risks
Internal control
Fraud
Cyber security
tools and techniques
Cyber risk reporting
Internal audit

Enterprise risk

risk management

RevisionCards

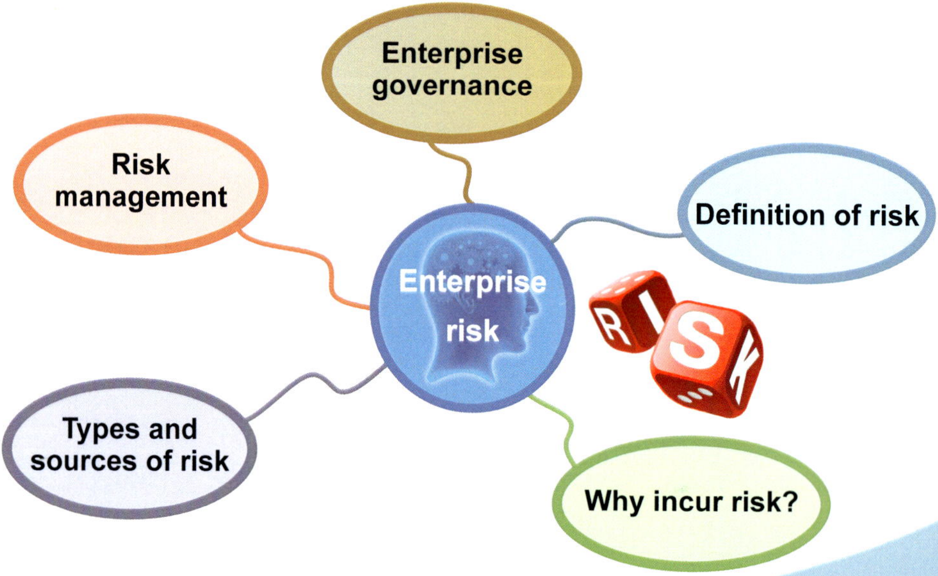
Enterprise governance
Risk management
Definition of risk
Enterprise risk
RISK
Types and sources of risk
Why incur risk?

Enterprise governance

A useful way of looking at the entire Risk Management (P3) syllabus is through the concept of Enterprise Governance.

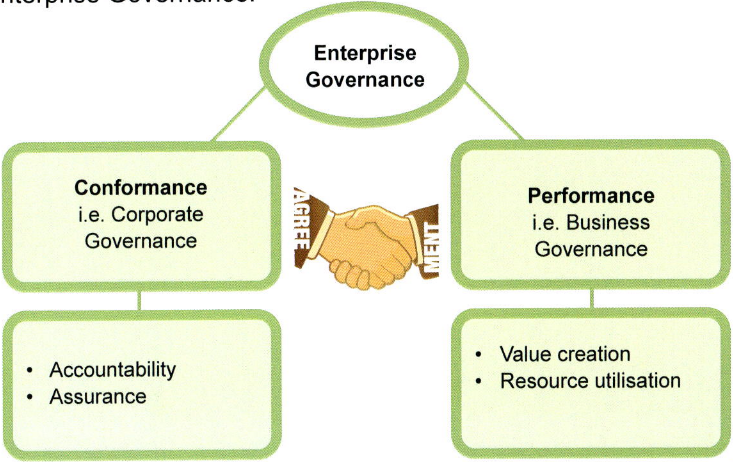

Definition of risk

Risk in business is the chance that future events or results may not be as expected.

Why incur risk ?

Incur risk to

- Gain competitive advantage
- Increase financial return

Types and sources of risk

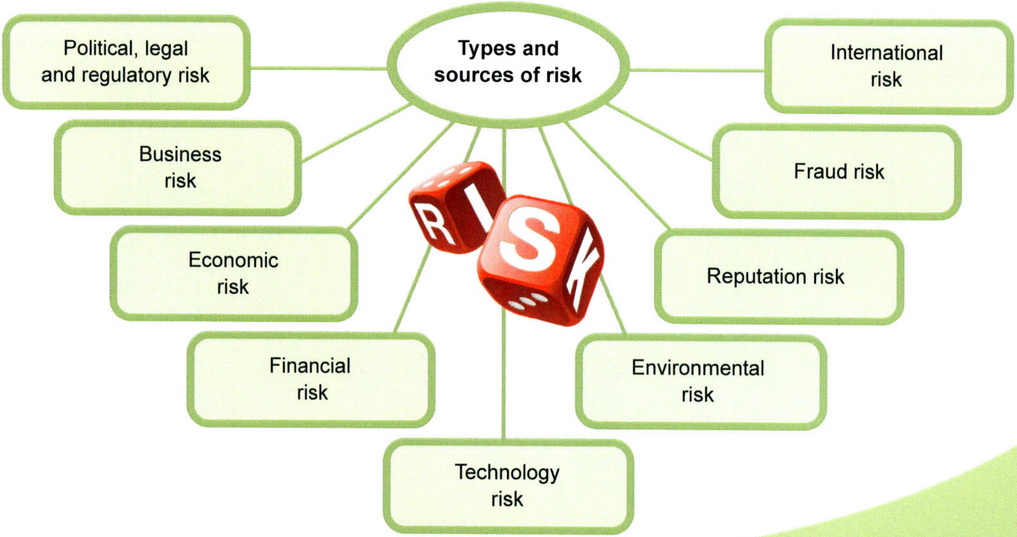

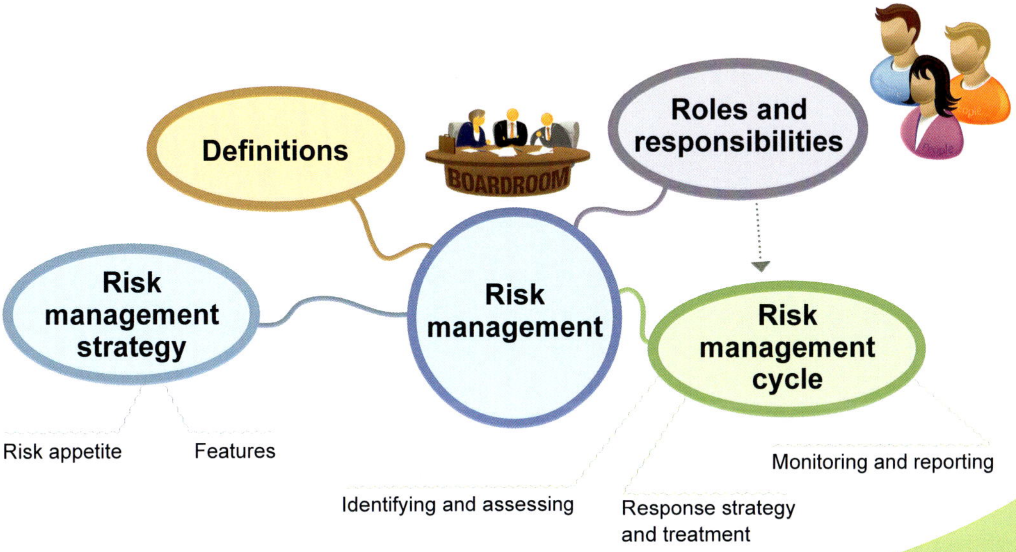
Definitions
BOARDROOM
Roles and responsibilities
Risk management strategy
Risk management
Risk management cycle
Risk appetite
Features
Identifying and assessing
Response strategy and treatment
Monitoring and reporting

Definitions

Risk management is defined as:

'the process of understanding and managing the risks that the organisation is inevitably subject to in attempting to achieve its corporate objectives'

CIMA's Official Terminology

Enterprise Risk Management (ERM) is defined as:

'a process, effected by an entity's board of directors, management and other personnel, applied in strategy setting and across the enterprise, designed to identify potential events that may affect the entity, and manage risk to be within its risk appetite, to provide reasonable assurance regarding the achievement of entity objectives.'

(COSO) (2003)

Risk appetite

Business strategy

Risk appetite
How much risk the business will accept

Risk strategy

Risk attitude
Overall approach to risk

Risk capacity
Maximum risk business can accept

Residual risk
Risk that cannot be managed

Risk management strategy features

Key features of a risk management strategy are:

- Responsibilities
- Attitude
- Performance criteria
- Appetite
- Objectives
- Culture
- Systems

Risk management cycle

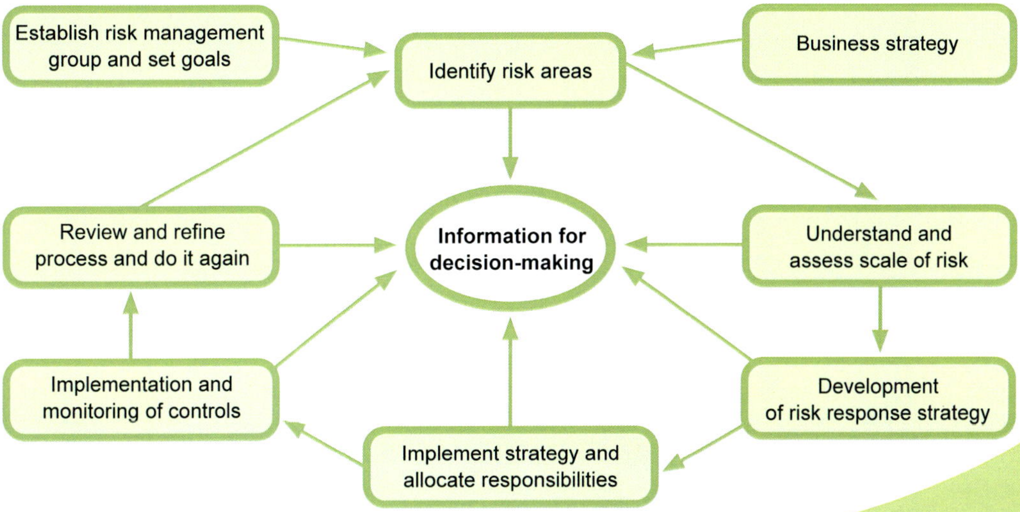

Risk management cycle: Identifying and assessing risks

Identifying risk

- Performed and controlled by risk committee
- Risks recorded in risk register
- Variety of methods such as brainstorming, internal audit inspections, external advisors, scenario planning

Assessing risk

QUANTIFYING

- Expected values
- Volatility
- Value at Risk (VaR)

RISK MAPPING

- Impact/ consequences
- Probability/ likelihood

Risk management cycle: Risk response strategy and treatment methods

Any risk response strategy aims to ensure that:

- Exposure to severe risks is minimised
- Unnecessary risks are avoided
- Appropriate measures of control are taken
- The balance between risk and return is appropriate

Risk map

		Impact/Consequence	
		Low	High
Probability/Likelihood	High	Reduce	Avoid
	Low	Accept	Transfer

Risk treatments (responses) include:

Reduce

Hedge

Diversify

Pool

Avoid

Transfer

Share

ISO 31000

- Risk assessment (including identification and evaluation)
- Risk treatment
- Monitoring and review
- Recording and reporting

ISO 31000 identifies the following risk treatments:

- Avoiding the risk
- Accepting the risk
- Removing the risk source
- Changing the probability
- Changing the outcome
- Sharing the risk
- Retaining the risk

Risk management cycle: Monitoring and reporting

A risk reporting system would include:

- System review of risk forecast
- Review of risk strategy and responses to significant risks
- Monitoring / feedback loop on action taken
- 'Early warning' system
- Incorporation of audit work

Risk reports show:

- **gross risk** = before the controls, transfer or management responses
- **net risk** (**residual risk**) = taking into account the controls, transfer and management responses

Roles and responsibilities

Who?	Responsibilities in relation to risk management
Board of directors	Ultimate responsibility Define risk appetite
Audit committee	Review internal control system
Risk committee	Risk management for whole company
Risk management group (led by Risk Manager)	Operational responsibility for risk management process

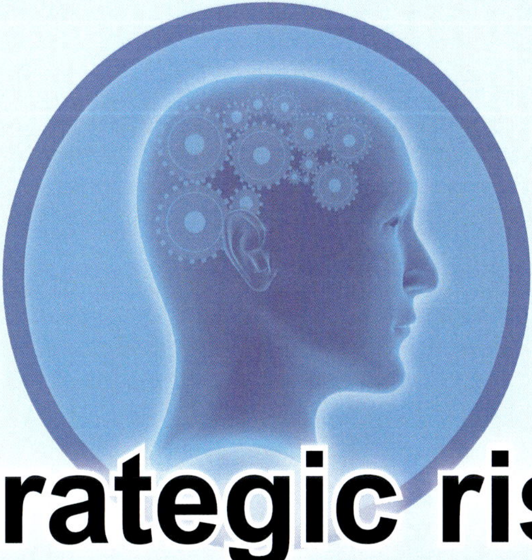

Strategic risk

risk management

RevisionCards

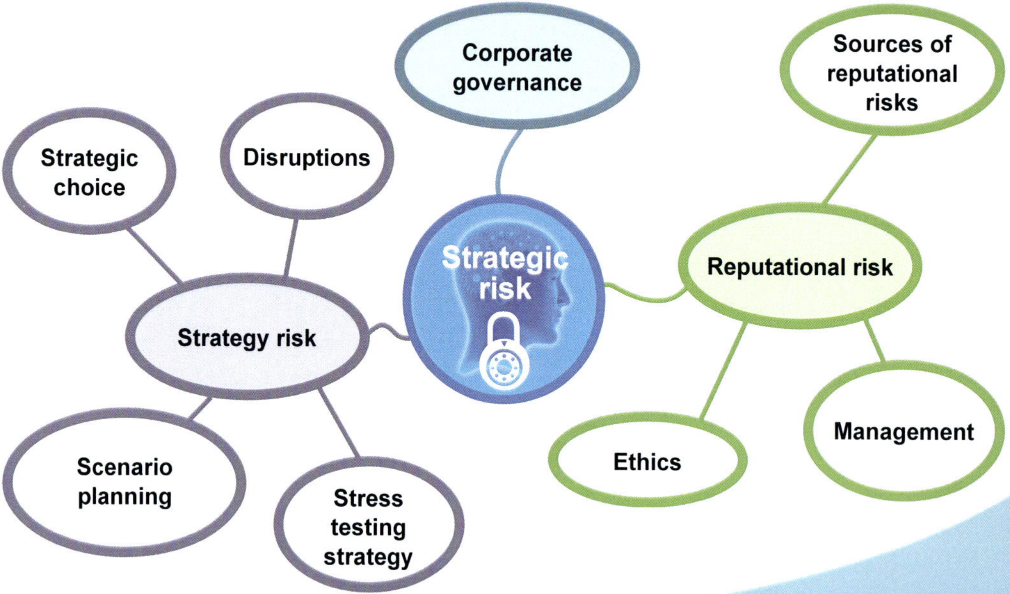
Corporate governance
Sources of reputational risks
Strategic choice
Disruptions
Strategic risk
Reputational risk
Strategy risk
Scenario planning
Stress testing strategy
Ethics
Management

Strategy risk

How do organisation choose the correct strategy, and what if they choose the wrong one?

Strategic choice:

Strategies must help organisations close the gap

The strategies must make each business unit competitive

Directions for growth – which products or markets should be focussed on?

How should expansion be achieved? Organic growth? Acquisition? Collaboration

Risks

Problems with the process of selecting strategy:

- too rigid
- lacks external focus
- not flexible enough in a dynamic industry
- not formal enough and fail to identify risks or cannot raise finance

Competitive advantage

Strategic scope		Competitive stance	
	Broad scope. Targets whole market	Cost leadership	Differentiation
	Narrow Scope. Targets one segment	Focus	

Competitive advantage – Risks

Cost leadership:

- Only room for one
- No fall back if position lost
- Constantly evolving to keep prices as low as possible

Differentiation:

- Need to innovate
- High costs – production, marketing
- Recession = hit hardest?

Focus:

- Finding an appropriate niche
- Success attracts competition
- Focus implies lower volumes so hard to keep costs low

Overall risks:

- Stuck in the middle?

Product/market strategy

Ansoff's matrix

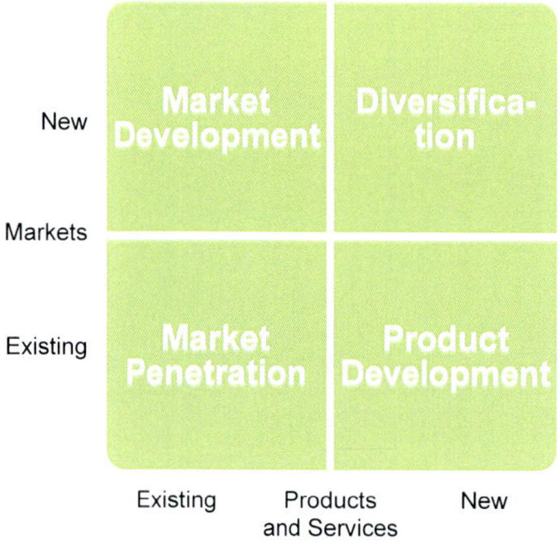

Product/market strategy – Risks!

Market penetration – is the least risky,

but lowest reward.

Product and market development – significant risk of failure here leading to reputation damage, costly entry and exit. They must be researched well.

Diversification – very risky, but if it works, significant reward.

- **Vertical integration** – the key risks are increased dependence on current market, more difficult to switch suppliers/distribution channels.
- **Conglomerate diversification** – leads to risks around lack of knowledge, skills, significant costs, failure (reputation).

Methods of growth – Risks!

Acquisition

- Costs
- Lack of understanding/knowledge
- Cultural issues
- IT intergration

Organic growth

- Time to get established
- Competitor reactions
- Lack of skills
- Effect on core operations

Collaboration

Types

- Joint venture
- Strategic alliance
- Franchising
- License
- Outsource

Risks (not specific to type)

- Strategic fit partner (reputation)
- Cost sharing
- Knowledge sharing
- Profit sharing
- Loss of control

Disruption

Disruptive innovation: a new product or service changes or creates a new market leading to existing products/services/ markets losing appeal. Usually involves technological advances.

Successful disruption:

- Simple
- Reducing the use of resources – environmentally friendly
- Cost – reductions!
- Accessibility
- Quality

Scenario Planning

- Using the risk register consider how the key risks, and other risks could develop over time.
- Consider implications for the organisation.
- Consider appropriate response.
- Revise and review as scenarios unfold.

Benefit = responding more quickly and appropriately than competition

Stress Testing

Identifying how an organisation would cope in difficult conditions.
Very popular for financial institutions since the credit crisis in 2008.

Considerations:

- **Focus** – Primary customer? How do you prioritise key stakeholder?
- **Measurement** – What KPIs? What boundaries?
- **Productivity/commitment** – How do you challenge norm? How committed are workforce?
- **Flexibility** – What uncertainties does your business face & how can you adapt?

Reputational risk:

Reputation is defined as the beliefs or opinions that are generally held about someone or something.

Reputational risk is therefore the likelihood of losses occurring due to a deterioration in the belief or opinion held about someone or something.

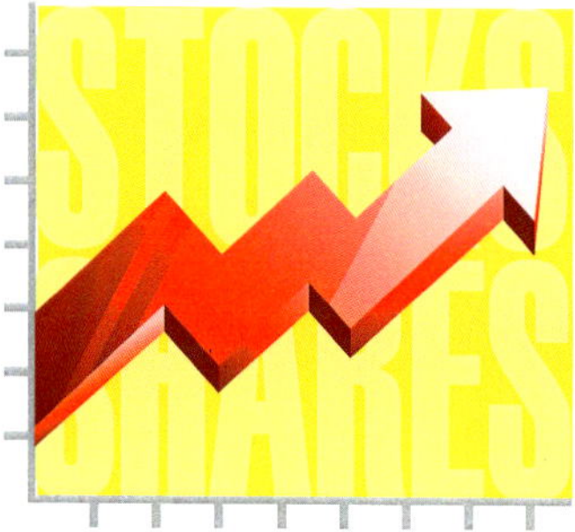

RISK MANAGEMENT – Strategic risk

Sources of reputational risks

- Unethical behaviour
- Transfer pricing
- Fraud
- Employees
- Managers
- Accounting
- Cyber security
- Data protection

Management

- Tone at the top
- Policies and procedures
- Training
- Recruitment
- Environmental awareness

ETHICS
A COMPANY
Fundamental ethical principles
Conflicts within employing organisation
Ethics
Ethical threats
Ethical conflict resolution

Fundamental principles

Confidentiality

Objectivity

Professional competence and due care

Integrity

Professional behaviour

Ethical conflict resolution

An ethical dilemma, or conflict, arises when one or more principles of the code are threatened.

1. Check facts
2. Escalate internally

3. Escalate externally
4. Refuse to remain associated with the conflict

Document the issue

Seek professional or legal advice

Conflicts within employing organisations

A professional accountant may be put under pressure to:

- Act contrary to law or regulation
- Act contrary to technical/professional standards
- Facilitate unethical/illegal earnings strategies
- Intentionally mislead others
- Issue a financial or non-financial report that materially misrepresents the facts

Safeguards to eliminate or reduce these threats include:

- Obtaining advice from within organisation, or professional body
- Existence of formal dispute resolution process
- Seeking legal advice

Ethical threats

CIMA's code of ethics identifies six categories of threat to the fundamental principles:

Self-interest	– as a result of financial or other interests
Self-review	– when previous judgement needs to be re-evaluated
Advocacy	– when a position is promoted to the point that objectivity may be compromised
Familiarity	– when a close relationship leads to a compromise of professional judgement
Intimidation	– actual or perceived threats deter objective action
Adverse interest	– member's interests are opposed to the employers

Corporate social responsibility (CSR)

CSR is an approach to business that considers all stakeholders and provides economic, social, environmental benefits along with sustainable growth for the organisation.

Benefits

Differentiation

Attracts and retains high calibre staff

Cost savings – reduced fines, less packaging, energy usage

New opportunities

Increased profitability – as a result of all of the above

Risks

Agency risk, directors choose the CSR aspects they like rather than the owners of the organisation

Loss of focus on primary aims

Spend too much

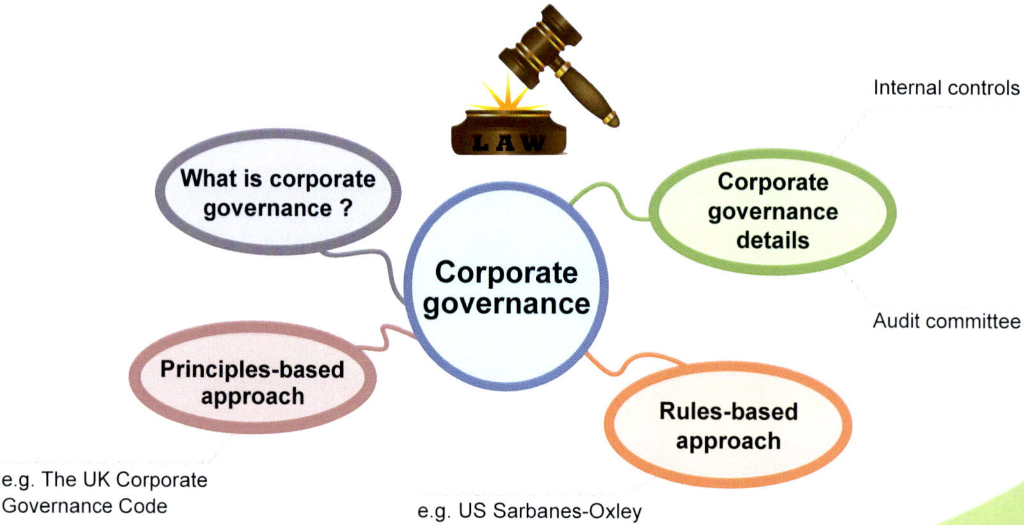
LAW
What is corporate governance ?
Corporate governance
Corporate governance details
Internal controls
Audit committee
Principles-based approach
e.g. The UK Corporate Governance Code
Rules-based approach
e.g. US Sarbanes-Oxley

What is corporate governance?

'the system by which companies are directed and controlled in the interest of shareholders and other stakeholders'

Importance of corporate governance:

- in most countries listed companies are required to comply
- it is often built into stock exchange listing rules – it seeks to prevent 'fat-cat salaries, plundering of the company pension fund, and other unethical behaviour...'

Limitations of corporate governance:

- it does not prevent company failure or collapse
- it cannot prevent companies failing to achieve their objectives

Principles-based approach e.g. The UK Corporate Governance Code

Board leadership and company purpose

Division of responsibilities

Composition, succession and evaluation

Audit, risk and internal control

Remuneration.

Rules-based approach e.g. US Sarbanes-Oxley (SOX)

A rules-based approach instills the corporate governance code into law with penalties for transgression (e.g. fines or imprisonment).

Corporate governance details

In relation to **internal controls** the **board** is responsible for

- **maintaining** a sound system of internal control
- **reviewing** the effectiveness of internal controls
- **reporting** to shareholders that this review has been carried out

(**Turnbull Report** provided more details)

Audit committees are required. These should

- have a minimum membership of three NEDs, or in the case of smaller companies, two NEDs
- monitor and review the effectiveness of the company's internal audit function or, where there is not one, consider annually whether there is a need for one and make a recommendation to the board

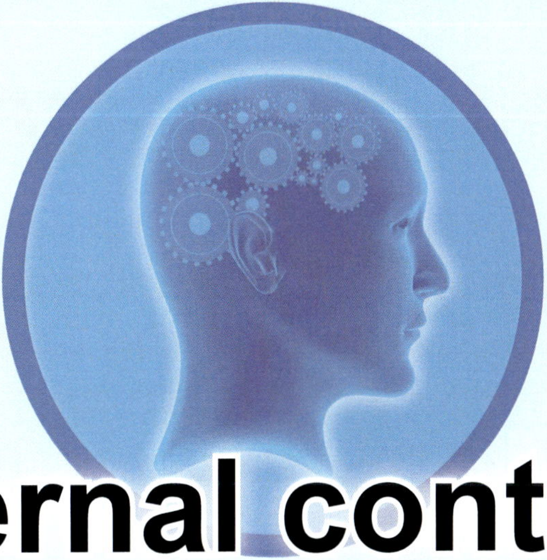

Internal controls

risk management

RevisionCards

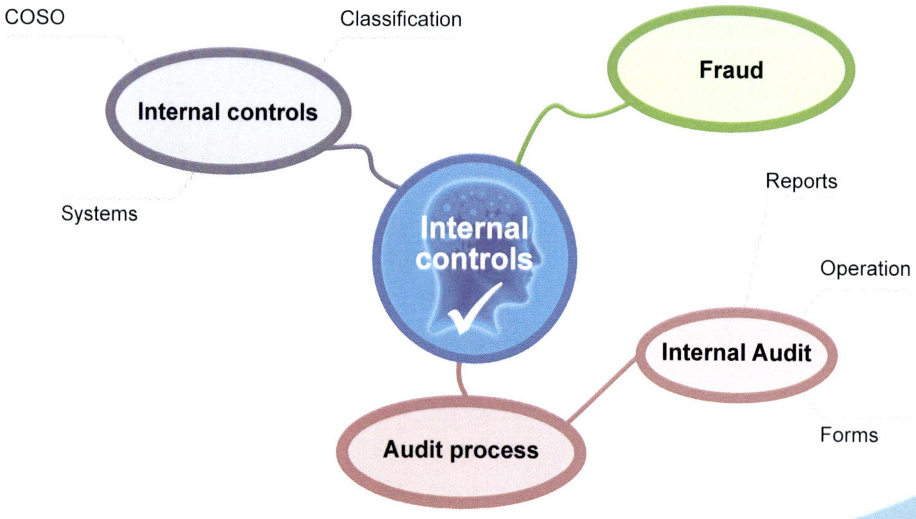
COSO
Classification
Internal controls
Systems
Fraud
Internal controls
Reports
Operation
Internal Audit
Forms
Audit process

Definition of an internal control system

The whole system of controls, financial and otherwise, established by the management in order to

- carry out the business of the enterprise in an orderly and efficient manner,
- ensure adherence to management policies,
- safeguard the assets,
- prevent and detect fraud and error, and
- secure as far as possible the completeness and accuracy of the records.

COSO model of effective internal control systems

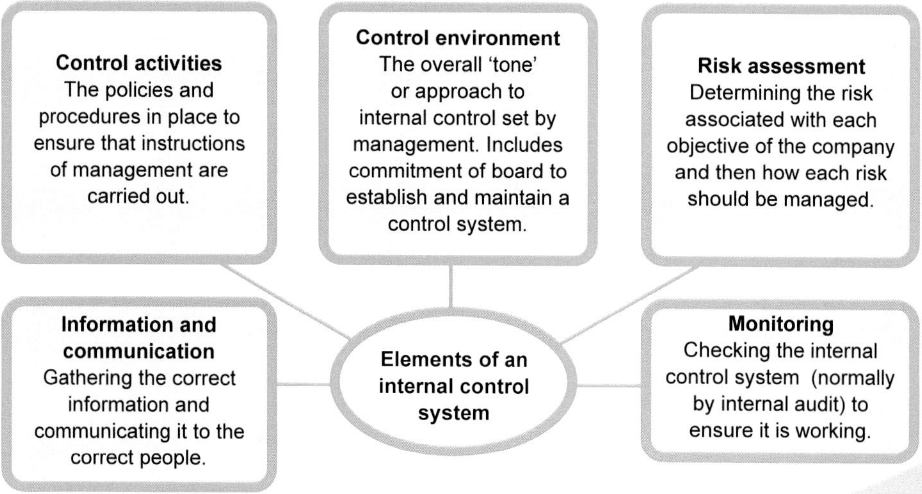

Classification of controls

Controls can be considered under three broad categories:

- Financial controls
- Non-financial quantitative controls
- Non-financial qualitative controls

Control activities include:

- Segregation
- Physical
- Authorisation
- Management
- Supervision
- Organisation
- Arithmetic and accounting
- Personnel

Fraud Prevention:

Whistleblowing

Anti-fraud culture

Risk awareness

Sound internal control system

Detection: It is not the auditors responsibility to detect fraud. It is the directors' and managements' responsibility.

Fraud Response:

Public Relations

Finance Director

HR

Police

Auditors

Insurance

Solicitor

Manager

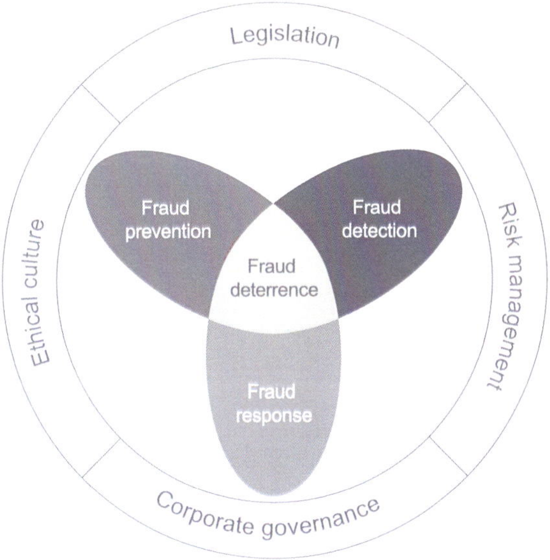

What is internal audit ?

Internal audit can be defined as 'an **independent appraisal** activity established within an organisation as a service to it. It is a control which functions by examining and evaluating the adequacy and effectiveness of other controls' (**CIMA**).

It is sometimes referred to as a **management review of controls**.

To protect the independence of the internal audit department the head of internal audit should have direct access to the audit committee.

Most work is carried out using a **risk-based approach**, concentrating audit effort on key risks.

Scope of internal audit

Sample testing

Compliance checks

Review accounting and internal control systems

E 3E's

Assist in external audit procedures

Minimise risk

Special investigations

Internal vs external audit

	External audit	Internal audit
Required by:	Statute 	Audit committee 
Responsibility:	To shareholders	To audit committee
Reports on:	Financial statements	Mainly internal controls
Forms opinion on:	True and fair view	Economy, efficiency and effectiveness of internal control system

External auditors take into account the work of internal audit when drawing up their audit plan, and assess the extent to which the findings of internal auditors can be relied upon.

Audit committee role

Review the financial statements

Review internal controls

Liase with internal audit

Liase with external audit

Types of audit work

Management

Value for money

Risk-based

Quality

Post completion

Transactions

Systems based

Compliance

Environmental and social

Audit process

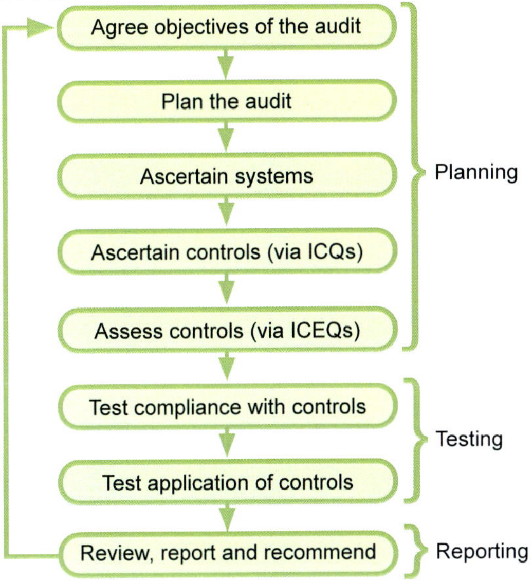

Types of testing

Types of audit testing

- **Compliance testing**
  - Test of controls
- **Substantive testing**
  - Test of balances or transactions
- **Analytical review (Substantive analytical procedures)**
  - Examination of ratios, trends and changes in balances
  - %

Cyber risks

risk management

RevisionCards

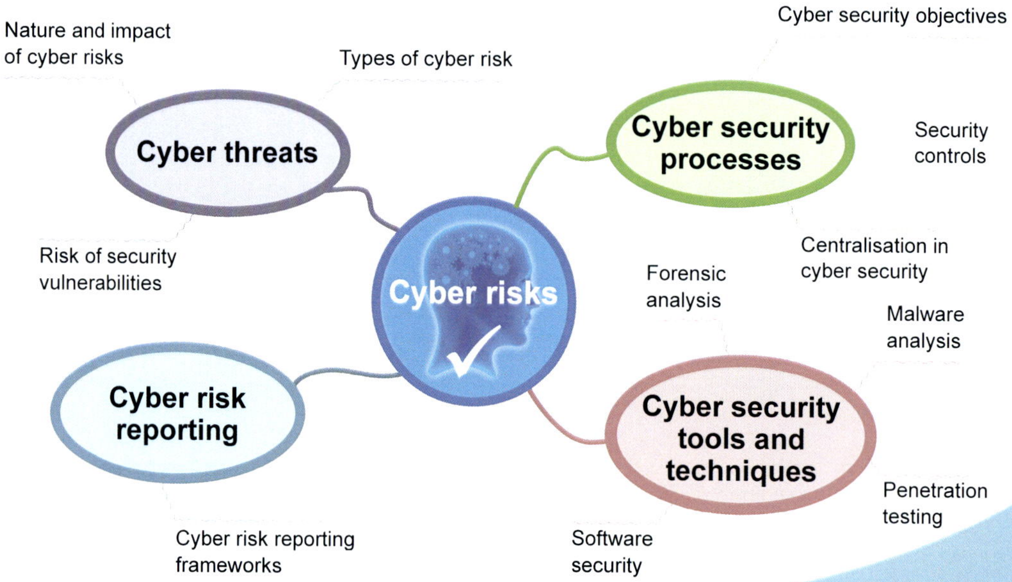
Nature and impact of cyber risks
Types of cyber risk
Cyber security objectives
Cyber threats
Cyber security processes
Security controls
Risk of security vulnerabilities
Cyber risks
Centralisation in cyber security
Forensic analysis
Malware analysis
Cyber risk reporting
Cyber security tools and techniques
Penetration testing
Cyber risk reporting frameworks
Software security

Cyber threats:

Nature and impact of cyber risks

Types of sensitive information

- PII (Name, address, DoB, CIMA ID number)
- Business info (confidential information about employees, business plans)
- Classified (government information, critical to national infrastructure)

Technology and organisation interaction

Examples include:

- ERPS
- Cloud
- Data centres
- VPN

Consideration of changes that affect cyber security like:

- Expansion
- Acquisition
- Internal restructure
- Regulatory changes

Security objectives

- Availability
- Confidentiality
- Integrity of data
- Integrity of processing

Change over methods

- Direct changeover
- Parallel running
- Pilot changeover
- Phased changeover

Types of cyber risk

Malware

- Ransomware
- Botnets
- Trojans
- Malvertising

Applications attacks

- DoS
- DDoS
- SQL injection
- Cross site scripting attacks (XSS attacks)

Hackers

- Ethical
- Unethical

Social engineering

- Phishing (SMS, email, phone calls)
- Spearphishing – targeted at an individual

Social media

Risks to firms

- Human error
- Productivity
- Data protection
- Reputation
- Inactivity

Risks to individual

- Trolling
- Physical theft
- Legal sanction
- Employability
- Permanence

Risk of security vulnerabilities

Technical – for example software defects
Procedural – for example poor system configuration, or not complying with company policy

Implications

- Downtime
- Reputation damage
- Customer flight
- Industry consequences
- Legal consequences

Cyber security processes:

Cyber security objectives

Cyber security risk governance

Roles – CIO, CISO, CTO, CRO as appropriate for the firm

Policies in place

Communication

- Internal – training, policies handbook, reminders
- External – policies for two way communication

Protection

What needs to be protected?

- Servers
- Desktops
- Laptops
- Mobile devices
- Networks
- Anything that stores data or connects to the network

How to protect it

- Policies/procedures – remote working, acceptable use, protection of PII
- Software updates – patch management
- Configurations – removal of unnecessary functionality
- Security products – antivirus software
- Application controls – input, processing, output

Forms of protection

- Identification – usernames, access codes
- Authentication – passwords, pin numbers, biometrics
- Authorisation – limit access within the systems
- Encryption
- Physical security – security guards, locks
- Training! Vital.

Certification – the digital handshake.

- SSL and TSL certificates

Detection

It is unrealistic to think that prevention will work, so organisations must be prepared and looking for a breach.

- Monitoring logs for unusual activity
- Applications that monitor networks
- Sharing intelligence

Response

Response teams to minimise losses and restore normal operations as quickly as possible.

Formal policies on:

- Business continuity planning
- Disaster recovery planning

Blockchain

A decentralised, distributed and public digital ledger used to record transactions across many computers so that the record cannot be altered without the consensus of the network.

Viewed as a benefit for cyber security given the public nature, rather than being closed and modified in private.

If anyone interferes with a transaction it will be rejected by the network.

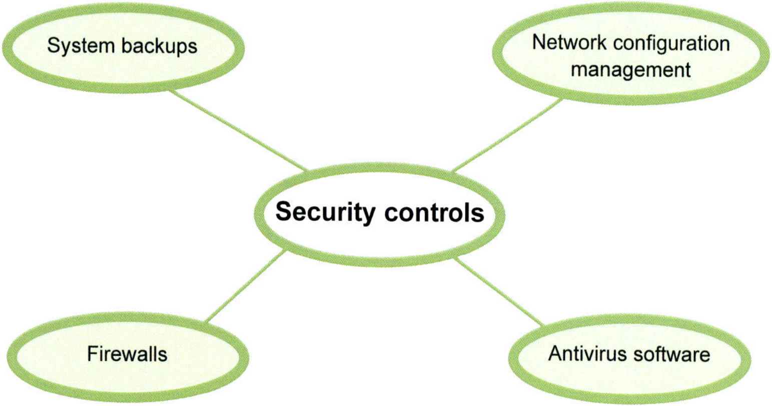
System backups
Network configuration management
Security controls
Firewalls
Antivirus software

Cyber security tools and techniques:

After an attack or breach has occurred the following 2 approaches help an organisation understand what happened and why, so they can defend against it better in the future.

Forensic analysis

After a breach has occurred:

- System level analysis – what part of the system has been affected
- Storage analysis – what has gone missing or public
- Network analysis – monitoring what data is moving across the network, looking for anomalys

Malware analysis

- Reverse engineering – deconstruct the malware to understand design
- Decompilation and disassembly
    - what was the purpose of the malware,
    - targeted or untargeted attack

Penetration testing

- Using white hat hackers to help understand vulnerabilities
- Network discovery – scope of the network
- Vulnerability probing – identify weakest links on a network
- Exploiting vulnerabilities – understand how the weak spots can be exploited
- Internal network penetration testing
- Web application penetration testing
- Wireless network penetration testing
- Simulated phishing testing

Software security

Security testing – internal controls
Software support from vendors
Effective patch mangament

Digital resilience

6 actions to integrate cyber security into business operations:

- Identify issues – what is at risk?
- Set a target- cybersecurity plan
- Delivery of the new system – change management
- Risk resource trade-offs – the right solution for organisation
- Aligns business and technology – both current operations and proposed
- Sustain the focus – everyone is involved!

Cyber risk reporting:

Cyber risk frameworks

AIC Triad

- Availiability
- Integrity
- Confidentiality

NIST cybersecurity framework

- Identify threats to an organisations systems and data
- Protect against threats
- Detect when a system has been breached
- Respond effectively to systems breaches
- Recover any compromised data and the systems affected

ISO270001

- Define a security policy
- Define the scope of the ISMS
- Conduct a risk assessment
- Manage identified risks
- Select control objectives and controls to be implemented
- Prepare a statement of applicability

AICPA Cyber Security Risk Management Reporting Framework

- Management's description
- Management's assertion
- The practitioner's opinion

RevisionCards

The Official Revision Cards are the only printed revision aids endorsed by CIMA. They provide complete coverage of the CGMA syllabus in bite-sized chunks and will help cement your knowledge and understanding.

Based upon research into learning styles and effective recall they:

- are highly visual and colourful which will be particularly effective for visual learners
- can be rearranged and reorganized so they will appeal to kinaesthetic learners who prefer to learn by doing
- reduce the content to the most important areas, making it far easier to digest and identify the relationships between key topics
- include handy exam tips and guidance on topic weighting.

Their small size makes them ideal for use anywhere, at home in the classroom or on the move.

2026 edition

Relevant for the CGMA professional qualification syllabus assessments

ISBN 978-1-83735-117-6

Kaplan Publishing UK
Unit 2, The Business Centre,
Molly Millars Lane,
Wokingham, Berkshire RG41 2QZ

Tel: +44 (0) 118 989 0629
Fax: +44 (0) 118 979 7455

Email: publishing@kaplan.co.uk
www.kaplanpublishing.co.uk

CIMA

Kaplan & the Environment

As we continually work to improve our sustainability credentials and reduce our impact, all of our books can now be 100% recycled with general household recycling

FSC
www.fsc.org
MIX
Paper | Supporting responsible forestry
FSC® C019717